Who \ Benedict Arnold?

by James Buckley Jr.

illustrated by Gregory Copeland

Penguin Workshop

For Carleigh and Vince—GC

PENGUIN WORKSHOP
An Imprint of Penguin Random House LLC, New York

Visit us online at www.penguinrandomhouse.com.

Library of Congress Control Number: 2020029355

ISBN 9780448488523 (paperback)   10 9 8 7 6 5 4 3 2 1
ISBN 9780593222720 (library binding)   10 9 8 7 6 5 4 3 2 1

Contents

Who Was Benedict Arnold?

On September 24, 1780, General Benedict Arnold was riding for his life. His horse galloped quickly through the trees following a steep path that headed toward the Hudson River, north of New York City. Benedict was one of the heroes of the Continental Army. He and his fellow colonists were fighting the American Revolutionary War, struggling for their freedom from Great Britain. Benedict had been a hero of several battles. Now, he was in terrible trouble.

As he rode, Benedict did not know how close his pursuers were. He kept his head down and guided his horse along the trail, his sword and pistols bouncing and clattering at his sides. He knew that a boat was waiting for him, and he hoped it would take him to safety on a larger ship waiting on the broad Hudson River.

He was probably thinking of his wife and four children, whom he had just left behind. He hoped they would all be safe. Benedict had met and married his wife when he was the American military governor of the city of Philadelphia, another important position he had held in service to his country.

But Benedict Arnold, once a Continental  Army hero, was not running away from British forces. Instead, he was fleeing his fellow American colonists. Just moments before Benedict made his quick escape on horseback, the leading Continental general, George Washington, had

George Washington

learned some terrible news: Benedict Arnold had sold plans for the American fort at nearby West Point to a British spy. He was a traitor!

When Washington got that sad news, he was only minutes away from arriving to meet with Benedict. But Benedict also had received a note. It said that the British spy Benedict had worked with had been caught. Benedict knew he had only one option—to run away. If the Continental Army caught up to him, he would be put on trial. As punishment for his crimes, he could be shot.

What had led a man who had once been a hero to turn on his nation? How did Benedict Arnold become one of the most hated men in US history? He had been a business owner, a ship captain, and a successful soldier and military leader. Now, he was a criminal.

When he reached the river's edge, Benedict pulled his horse to a stop and leaped off. He shouted at the sailors waiting by the small boat to pull him quickly away from the shore. He was heading to the safety that he could only find aboard a British ship. Benedict would never find a safe home in America again.

CHAPTER 1
An Active Early Life

Benedict Arnold was born on January 14, 1741, in the British colony of Connecticut. Like everyone in the town of Norwich, he was a subject of the king of England. Great Britain owned Connecticut and twelve other colonies in North America. They spread along the Atlantic coast from what is now Maine in the north to Georgia in the south.

Benedict's family was one of the wealthiest in Norwich. His father, also named Benedict, owned ships that traded between islands in the Caribbean and the American colonies. His mother, Hannah, was a well-respected leader in their church. Benedict had three younger sisters, Hannah, Mary, and Elizabeth.

The family was well known. Their seats in church were those reserved for the most important members of the congregation.

Young Benedict led a very active life. He was a leader among his group of friends, often deciding what they would do or choosing where they would go. They often played in the nearby woods, camping or hunting. He became an excellent ice skater, zipping over frozen ponds and rivers.

He had learned to read and write in a one-room schoolhouse. But when he was not in school, he had many adventures. Benedict would sometimes try dangerous things just to get attention. Once, he jumped onto a moving waterwheel. This was a huge wooden device that spun on the side of a building. Part of the wheel went underwater as it turned. Inside the building, the wheel was connected to a millstone that ground wheat into flour. As people watched in shock, Benedict clung to the wheel and rode it all the way around, holding on as it passed underwater. He popped

back out, soaking wet and grinning. People were shocked that he would do something so bold and daring.

One summer, he sailed by ship with his father to other colonies and even traveled as far as the Caribbean Sea, stopping at Saint Kitts, Martinique, and the Cayman Islands.

When Benedict was eleven, he was sent to a boarding school in nearby Canterbury. He studied Latin and math, as well as Greek and the Bible. While he was away at school, he once again showed his daring side. At a dock nearby, he climbed high up on a ship's mast before the crew could catch him.

Britain's Colonies

In the 1700s, the nation of Great Britain owned colonies—land that they controlled—all over the world. Some British colonies were in India, Asia, and Africa. In North America, Great Britain owned part of Canada as a colony.

Great Britain also controlled a large number of islands in the Caribbean Sea, collectively called the British West Indies. They included what are now Bermuda, the Bahamas, the British Virgin Islands, Saint Kitts, Martinique, the Cayman Islands, Barbados, and others.

Great Britain also owned the thirteen colonies that eventually would become the United States: Virginia, Massachusetts Bay, New Hampshire, Maryland, Connecticut, Rhode Island and Providence Plantation, Delaware, North Carolina, South Carolina, New York, New Jersey, Pennsylvania, and Georgia.

British colonies in America and the Caribbean

Then, from this high spot, he dove into the water to escape. Later, the school's headmaster wrote to Benedict's mother about another incident. When a barn caught fire, Benedict ran into the burning building. He climbed to the roof and walked along the top as the smoke and flames grew around him.

During his second year at boarding school, Benedict got sad news from home. His sisters Mary and Elizabeth had died from yellow fever. Hannah had been very sick, too, but she had survived. Benedict's mother told him not to come home because she feared he might also catch the deadly illness.

Everything really began to change for Benedict in 1754. His father's business had been slowly losing money. Eventually, the family's money ran out, and Benedict had to return to Norwich from his boarding school. The Arnolds were no longer among the town's leading families. Benedict was often teased by other kids because of his family's troubles. He fought with the boys who made fun of him. He also had to take care of his father, who sometimes drank too much. It was embarrassing

for thirteen-year-old Benedict. He became more and more upset about what people might think of him and his family.

During the fall of 1754, Benedict met some Mohegan people who lived nearby. They taught him how to paddle a canoe and move silently through the woods. He learned to fish and hunt. His adventures in the rivers and forests of Connecticut were not enough for Benedict, though.

He still got into trouble for doing dangerous things, like once starting a huge bonfire. Finally, he was caught by a constable, a type of policeman. Benedict threatened to hit the officer! This was too much for Mrs. Arnold. She arranged for her angry, active boy to go to work as an apprentice. He needed to find something positive to do with his time, and she needed him to settle down and help his family.

In the American colonies, many young people worked as apprentices, learning a job or a skill by helping an expert. Apprentices worked in shops or in stables, for candle makers, blacksmiths, and in many other businesses. They often did the hardest or dirtiest tasks.

Being an apprentice was a job, and it came with many rules. Apprentices had to work for little or no pay for many years while they learned a particular skill or craft. The business owner or expert craftsman paid for their food and a place to live but usually made the apprentice work long hours. At the end of their time, however, they hoped to have the skills to open their own businesses.

In 1755, when he was fourteen, Benedict became an apprentice with the Lathrop family. The Lathrops owned an apothecary, a store that

sold medicines, bandages, and herbs. Benedict was put to work in the shop, packing boxes and learning everything about the business. The Lathrops also sold other products like cloth, wine, and tobacco.

Work seemed to change Benedict. Once he had used his youthful energy for playing pranks and having fun; now, he put his energy into becoming rich.

CHAPTER 2
B. Arnold, Shopkeeper

Benedict worked long hours at the Lathrops' shop. He learned about the medicines they sold and what sort of cloth was most popular among customers. As he grew in the job, the Lathrops gave him a little money. He often used it to buy fancy shoes, which he loved.

In 1759, his mother and the Lathrops gave Benedict permission to join the British Army. He trained with a group of soldiers that was preparing to march against Fort Ticonderoga in upper New York State in what was known in the colonies as the French and Indian War. They marched and practiced their drills and worked in camp but never fought in a battle.

While he was there, he got word that his mother was very sick, and he returned to Norwich to be with her. Benedict remained in Connecticut to help care for his mother and returned to his apprenticeship. But Benedict's mother died in August 1759. He was just eighteen years old.

The Lathrops eventually began sending Benedict on short trips to the British-controlled West Indies to learn more about trading, buying, and selling. But back in Norwich, Benedict's father continued to get into trouble for his debts and drinking. Benedict often had to help him, too.

In 1761, Benedict's father died. He didn't leave Benedict and his sister, Hannah, very much money. However, about the same time, Benedict completed his apprenticeship. The Lathrops believed in him and loaned him money to start his own shop. Benedict and Hannah moved to New Haven, a larger town about sixty miles from Norwich.

Benedict set sail for London, England, from the port of New Haven. There, he bought hundreds of items, including cloth, tea, books, maps, and medicine to fill his Connecticut shop.

Most he bought on credit. He promised to pay for the goods after he earned the money by selling them.

When he returned to New Haven, he put up a sign on his store that read, "B. Arnold, Druggist, Bookseller, etc. from London." He loved wearing some of the fancy new clothes he had brought from London. He rode in an expensive horse-drawn cart. He chose a Latin motto for himself: *Sibi Totique* which means "for self and all." Benedict must have believed that making himself happy should be his most important goal.

Benedict ran his shop well, but he made a few mistakes. He did not pay back many of the people in London who had given him merchandise on credit for his store. Even though he was earning a living from his shop, he was not honest with the people who had loaned him money and products. At that time, if you did not pay your debts, you could be put in jail. In 1763, Benedict was jailed for six weeks. He was allowed out after paying back only a small portion of what he owed.

However, even after spending time in jail, Benedict still seemed to look at making money as the most important thing in life.

CHAPTER 3
Adventure at Sea

For his next business adventure, Benedict sold the Norwich home that his father had left him and used the money to buy a ship called *Fortune*.

Benedict was now Captain Arnold, international merchant. His ship carried wood, horses, oats, and clothing to the islands of the West Indies in the Caribbean Sea. He traded those goods for gold, salt, sugar, rum, and molasses to sell back in Connecticut.

Sometimes, he even traveled north to Canada to sell his goods.

At this time, merchants such as Benedict had to pay taxes, sometimes called *duty*, on the goods they carried. The taxes went to the British government because they owned the colonies. Benedict, like many traders, did his best to avoid paying these taxes. He would land at places where he didn't think there were any tax collectors, or he would disguise his cargo by covering it up, hiding it in secret places in his ship, or by mislabeling it to fool the tax collectors. He was trying to keep more of his profits by paying fewer taxes than he owed.

Benedict opposed the taxes on shipping, and he was not alone. Throughout the American colonies, more and more people were objecting to the tax laws of Great Britain. They did not like paying money to the government of King George III, who lived an ocean away. American colonists began to think the taxes were unfair.

King George III

Britain's Stamp Act of 1765 was especially hard on the American colonists. That law forced them to buy stamps to place on any kind of paper, including books, newspapers, and legal documents. It even included playing cards! The stamps showed that a tax had been paid. Products without stamps were not supposed to be sold. In

New Haven, Benedict joined a group called the Sons of Liberty and took part in protests against the British taxes.

Some stamps from the Stamp Act of 1765

Benedict continued to try to earn a living in trading and shipping. In 1767, when he was twenty-six, he married Margaret Mansfield. In the next few years, they had three sons—Benedict, Richard, and Henry. Margaret had some help with the boys from Benedict's sister, Hannah.

Benedict was away from home much of the time. In a letter to Margaret, he complained that she did not write him often enough. "I assure you I think it hard [to believe] that you have wrote me only once when there have been so many opportunities."

Margaret Mansfield

Sons of Liberty

The Sons of Liberty was a group of American colonists who protested unfair laws and taxes put on the colonies by Great Britain. They tried to make life difficult for their English rulers. Sons of Liberty groups were formed in Boston, New York City, Connecticut, and other northeast colonies. They held rallies, staged protests, and even attacked British officials. To protest the new taxes of the Stamp Act of 1765, they stole the paper that was to be taxed and destroyed it.

The Sons of Liberty's most famous protest was the Boston Tea Party in 1773.

Members of the group boarded British ships in Boston Harbor. Angry about new taxes demanded by Great Britain, they threw tea that had been shipped from England into the water. Samuel

Adams and John Hancock were among the group's
most famous members.

By 1773, Benedict stopped sailing and settled down to run the store in New Haven. His problems continued, however. As a way to get back at the British government for charging taxes, Benedict and his fellow Sons of Liberty began to attack the American colonists known as Tories, who supported King George III.

In 1774, colonists up and down the east coast were becoming upset with the British, who were moving their troops in to prepare for a fight. It looked more and more as if war between Britain and its North American colonies was coming. That December, the patriots of New Haven—the men who wanted to rebel against the British—banded together. They formed their own militia (an organized group of armed men) to fight for the patriot cause. They chose Benedict as their captain. He began to bring together the company, teaching them how to march together, carry guns, and dress like soldiers. He wore an officer's coat with fancy lapels, white britches (pants that end just past the knee), and tall black leather boots.

In April 1775, word came to New Haven from Massachusetts of the first shots fired in what became known as the Revolutionary War. Benedict, always ready for an adventure, decided to march to the fighting. He asked the man in charge of New Haven's guns and gunpowder to turn them all over to him. At first the man said no,

but Benedict forced him to hand over the key to the needed supplies. "None but Almighty God shall prevent my marching!" he yelled as he demanded the gunpowder.

Benedict led his men out of town, finally heading for battle near Cambridge, Massachusetts. But this time, he would fight *against* the British.

CHAPTER 4
Off to War

The American colonists gathered near Cambridge to plan their attacks against the British. In late spring 1775, Benedict arrived there with his New Haven troops and an idea. He had seen Britain's Fort Ticonderoga in upper New York during several of his sailing trips. He proposed to Massachusetts military leaders that he attack that fort and capture its cannons, guns, and gunpowder. The Americans had very few supplies of their own. The Massachusetts Committee of Public Safety was the first group organizing attacks, and they gave Benedict permission to try his plan. They gave him a promotion to colonel, but they kept his Connecticut soldiers in Massachusetts.

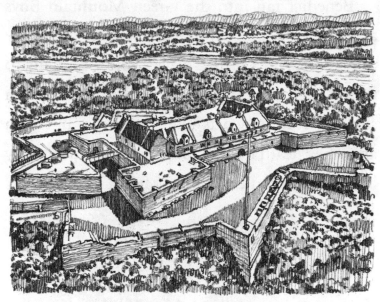

Fort Ticonderoga

Benedict headed immediately toward the fort, eager to gather men to make an attack. He quickly discovered that he was not the only American with this plan. Ethan Allen was a rebel leader in Vermont. He was in charge of the Green Mountain Boys, a group of woodsmen who were also skilled fighters. Allen and his men had also been given orders to capture Fort Ticonderoga.

Benedict ran into the Green Mountain Boys at a tavern in Castleton, Vermont. At first, they thought he was a British officer who was trying to recruit them to join the British army, since such soldiers wore red coats like Benedict's. But even after they heard he was an American patriot, they laughed and said they already had a leader. It was

a very tense meeting. Benedict tried to boss the men around, but they ignored him. Benedict had official orders but no soldiers. Allen had men, but his orders had come from a different colonial group. Eventually, Allen agreed to let Benedict join him and share command of the group.

Ethan Allen (1738–1789)

Ethan Allen was born in Connecticut and moved north, where he bought land in what would later become Vermont. Neighboring New York colony owners tried to take the land back. That led Ethan to form the Green Mountain Boys—a group of fighting woodsmen who protected their lands against other colonists.

During the American Revolution, Ethan led his men into the fight. After several battles in 1775, they rode north to attack Montreal, Canada. Ethan was captured during an unsuccessful battle and held prisoner by the British.

After the war ended, Ethan tried to help convince Congress to let Vermont join the United States. He died two years before that wish came true in 1791.

Very early in the morning on May 10, 1775, Benedict, Ethan, and the Green Mountain Boys waited outside Fort Ticonderoga. After hearing the signal, they all ran toward it, shouting loudly. Benedict reached the gate of the fort first. A British guard shot at him and missed.

Benedict swung his sword and knocked the man down. The Green Mountain Boys poured into the fort behind their leaders.

The British soldiers were all asleep. The Americans took over the fort in minutes, without a fight. Ethan's men began their victory celebration by drinking the rum they had found at Ticonderoga. Benedict tried to take control but had little success. After a few days, most of the Vermont men had left, and Benedict's men from Connecticut had arrived. The former shopkeeper was in command of the fort, a winner in his first battle against the enemy.

He added another victory shortly after. Though he had no orders to do so, Benedict captured a British ship on Lake Champlain, north of Ticonderoga. He then sailed that ship even farther north with some of his Connecticut soldiers, and they attacked a British post in St. John's, Canada.

But by the time the group returned to Fort Ticonderoga, another colonial officer had arrived and been put in charge. Benedict was very upset and offended. He decided to return to New Haven and took his men with him. When he arrived, he was told that his wife, Margaret, had died. His sister, Hannah, had been taking care of his sons.

And then Benedict received even more bad news. This time it came from the Continental Congress—the group that was running the colonies in the early days of the Revolutionary War.

Benedict had sent a bill to the Continental Congress for the money he'd spent on his men and his mission. They decided to pay Benedict back only part of the money, not all that he had spent. Benedict was not happy. He felt the colonial leaders had not given him enough credit for his part in the capture of Fort Ticonderoga. Once again, he was upset with how he was being treated.

CHAPTER 5
A Daring Trip to Canada

By late summer 1775, Benedict wanted to get back to the fighting. Even though he felt insulted by the Continental Congress, he wanted another chance at glory and success. General George Washington had taken over command of the colonies' Continental Army. He had heard about Benedict's role in capturing Fort Ticonderoga, and he gave him an important mission: Benedict was ordered to lead over one thousand men on a long march north to invade the British colonial city of Quebec in Canada.

Benedict gathered his men and supplies. They built more than two hundred flat-bottomed boats that he hoped the group could use to cross the rivers and lakes along the way. Not long after the journey began, the boats had to be abandoned. The uncharted land was too hilly and thick with trees for the men to carry them. And the rivers were too dangerous.

Flat-bottomed boats called bateaux

For weeks, the men marched and camped. The weather was awful—cold, windy, rainy, and snowy. They ran low on food and had to eat shoe leather, soap, and even their dogs. Benedict urged his men to keep moving, but many deserted and went home.

Finally, after more than two months of those terrible conditions, Benedict was able to get his men to Quebec. But they still had to fight. Since Benedict had fewer men than the British, he and his aides waited until a big blizzard hit the area before attacking the Quebec fort.

On December 31, under the cover of snow, they charged. The British fired cannons and shot muskets. The Americans had only the muskets and pistols they could carry. Many Americans died. The attack went on for a day, until Benedict was hit in the leg by a musket ball. Bleeding badly, he was carried from the field. The American forces had to retreat.

For more than three months, the Americans surrounded the British fort but could not break through. Finally, Benedict decided that his troops had to leave. At a nearby lake, they climbed aboard ships that had been sent by the Continental Army. As the leader, but still limping from his wound,

Benedict was the last American soldier to step off Canadian soil for the journey south.

When Benedict returned to New Haven, some people in the Continental Army leadership gave him credit for his long march and brave attempt to take the Quebec fort. But others criticized him for taking military supplies after the battle and selling them. He also had arguments with other officers about the Canadian battles.

He even wrote to Congress again, complaining that he had given "my ease, health, and a great part of my private property" to help the war effort, and he was not being treated well in return.

However, the war continued and leaders were needed. In 1776, Washington again called on Benedict, this time because of his sailing and shipbuilding skills. The British were threatening to sail south through Lake Champlain to capture parts of the northern colonies. Benedict ordered more than a dozen small ships built on the southern shore of the lake.

When the fleet was assembled, he led it out to face the much larger British fleet. A fierce battle followed. Cannonballs smashed into the American ships, and the Americans tried to fight back with cannons of their own. Ships burned and sank, while men on both sides were killed by flying splinters of wood or by being blown overboard.

Benedict's ships were trapped behind a small island, and he knew that another battle might destroy them all, so he created a plan to sneak out past the British at night, after the fighting would have stopped for the day. At nightfall, his ships put out all their lights and slowly and quietly slipped away, one after another. As the last ships left the shelter of the island, the British saw what was happening and began to fire. But it was too late. Most of the remaining American ships got away safely. To save the rest, Benedict set his own ship on fire and fled in a smaller boat.

The British could not sail safely past the flaming ship.

The battle seemed like a loss for the Americans, but Benedict's strategies on the water had kept the enemy from moving farther south on the lake. Soon, winter came and the British, too, had to retreat.

CHAPTER 6
Saratoga

In the winter after the battle on Lake Champlain, Benedict got more bad news from Congress. They had promoted five other officers, even though he had served longer than any of them. That meant that they were ranked higher than Benedict, a brigadier general. He felt that this was very unfair. He tried to get Congress to

change its mind, but he was unsuccessful. Some members of Congress did not like how Benedict was acting. They wanted him to be more respectful of their authority.

At the same time, a former officer named John Brown had become very upset with the way Benedict behaved, both on and off the battlefield.

Brown accused Benedict of many crimes and printed a letter that read, in part, "Money is this man's god and to get enough of it, he would sacrifice his country." Benedict was so upset by Congress and by Brown that he wanted to resign from the army.

But a few days later, Benedict was once again called to lead American soldiers. They were defending Ridgefield, a town near Norwich. He rode his horse at the head of his men, and they fought off the British troops. At one point, Benedict's horse was shot and killed! As the horse fell, Benedict was trapped beneath it.

A British solider saw his struggle and tried to take Benedict prisoner. Benedict pulled out his pistol, shot the man, and escaped.

After his bravery at Ridgefield, Washington gave Benedict another important assignment near Saratoga, in the colony of New York. He was assigned to assist two generals planning a major attack on British troops there.

As the day of battle at Saratoga neared, he began to argue with General Horatio Gates, the leader of the Continental Army forces there. The arguments grew so fierce that General Gates ordered Benedict to remain in camp instead of going to the battlefield.

Horatio Gates

On September 19, the first Battle of Saratoga began. Benedict was forced to listen to the far-off gunfire from his tent. He wished he could be a part of the action. At one point, he ordered reserve troops that had remained in camp into the fight. General Gates reversed that order and sent them back. Benedict believed that the general was not fighting hard enough. Late in the day, he jumped onto a horse and rode off, calling out, "By God, I'll put an end to it!"

But Gates forced Benedict to return. As darkness fell on the first day, the outcome of the battle was in doubt. For two weeks, the opposing armies faced each other with little action. The British were running out of supplies and would have to move soon. General Gates was happy to just sit and wait. Benedict wanted action.

Finally, on October 7, 1777, the British made moves to attack. Without waiting for orders, Benedict took a chance and charged onto the field on his horse. Screaming and yelling, he urged the Americans forward. Bullets flew around him, but he kept riding and encouraging his men. For nearly an hour, he led charge after charge. Finally, a bullet smashed into Benedict's left leg. Another went into his horse, killing it. The horse fell, landing on Benedict's wounded leg.

The British surrender at Saratoga, 1777

The fighting raged on, but Benedict's inspired leadership had made the difference. The British retreated in panic, and the Americans won an important battle.

The Continental Army soon returned to Boston, where they were greeted by large, happy crowds. The soldiers marched their British prisoners into town while Americans cheered their victorious army. Benedict, meanwhile, was being looked after by doctors who feared they might have to cut off his injured leg. Benedict refused to let them. It took him several months to begin to recover. His injured left leg was now two inches shorter than his right, and he would limp for the rest of his life.

In May, he finally made it home to New Haven. The grateful citizens gave him a parade. Ships in the harbor fired their cannons in celebration. Congress finally awarded him a new rank: major general. He was now equal to the men who had once been above him. Benedict, it seemed, could finally feel good about his service to his country.

CHAPTER 7
Trouble in Philadelphia

Benedict's injured leg prevented him from heading back into battle, at least for a while. In the summer of 1778, Washington appointed him the military governor of Philadelphia. The job put Benedict in charge of American civilians and troops living in the city, which had only recently been taken back from British control. Soon, some of Benedict's bad habits returned in Philadelphia.

He took British goods and supplies captured by American troops and sold them, keeping the money for himself. The local leaders didn't like how well he treated the Tory citizens, whom the patriots hated. And they really did not approve when he fell in love with Peggy Shippen, the daughter of a leading British merchant. Benedict and Peggy were engaged in early 1779.

Peggy Shippen

Benedict was angry at how he had been treated by Congress. He believed they still owed him money from earlier years and that they had questioned his honor by not promoting him fast enough.

And Benedict believed that as military governor, he should live in fine style. He borrowed money to buy one of the city's largest houses.

Benedict and Peggy's mansion, Mount Pleasant

He also had a carriage built that looked like a chariot, which he used to tour the city.

Joseph Reed, who soon became the president of Pennsylvania (an office like a governor), took a

huge dislike to Benedict.
Reed disagreed strongly
with how Benedict was
behaving in his new
role in Philadelphia.

Joseph Reed

In February 1779,
Reed charged Benedict
with serious crimes,
that included using
public wagons for his
own use, issuing illegal passes to British citizens,
and generally treating patriot citizens poorly.
Reed demanded that Congress and George
Washington put Benedict on trial.

While these charges against him dragged
on, Benedict and Peggy were married in April
1779. By this time, his sister, Hannah, and
Benedict's three boys were all living with him in
Philadelphia, too. He had a large family to take
care of, and he wanted to make sure he appeared

to be wealthy and successful. But he was only earning his military governor's salary.

Continuing to believe that he was being mistreated by the American government and now by American colonists in Philadelphia,  Benedict wrote a letter to John André, who was then stationed in New York City. André was a British officer who worked directly for General Sir Henry Clinton, one of the leaders of the British Army in America.

John André

In the letter, Benedict referred to himself with a code name: Monk. But it was clear to André who Monk really was.

In the letter, Benedict asked if he might be able to offer anything to the British in return for money and a position in the British Army. This was a terrible act of treason—the crime of betraying your country. To many people in America, Benedict was still considered a patriot and a hero. Yet by starting this plan, he was turning his back on the colonists and thinking only of himself.

CHAPTER 8
Discussions with a Spy

André received Benedict's first letter and realized that he had something very valuable. If he could really get the famous Benedict Arnold, hero of Ticonderoga and Saratoga, to help the British, it might help them win the war.

André began writing to Benedict. Because they both knew that their letters might be read by others, they disguised what they wrote. André taught Benedict how to write in lemon juice between the lines of a letter written in ink. The lemon juice was invisible, but André could read it by holding it up to a candle. Such letters had an F in one corner, to let the reader know to use fire to see the hidden message.

For other letters, the men wrote in code.

Communicating in Code

People have used many types of code for thousands of years. It is a way to disguise what you are writing so that only a few people can understand the true message. It is important to know the "key" to the code.

Mask code

John André and Benedict Arnold often used a "book" code. Both had a copy of the exact same book, a popular British dictionary. They would write a series of numbers that stood for the page, line, and number of the word in that line. Only someone who had the right book could figure out which words the numbers meant.

A "mask" code was also used by Revolutionary War spies. A person receiving a letter would place another piece of paper on top of the letter. The top paper would have holes cut into it in a specific pattern. The words that showed through the holes revealed the secret message.

Benedict asked André for money in return for secrets about the Continental Army. After getting General Clinton's approval, André agreed to the deal. The letters detailing their plans went back and forth between the two men for months.

Meanwhile, the trial for the charges against Benedict made by Reed in Philadelphia finally occurred near Christmas 1779. Benedict spoke strongly in his own defense. During the trial,

he claimed that, "My conduct from the earliest period of this war to the present time has been steady and uniform." Yet even as he said this, he was trying to sell America's secrets to the British.

In late January 1780, Benedict was declared innocent of several of the charges but guilty of two others: He had illegally used army horses and wagons to carry his goods, and he had also given a pass to a ship that turned out to be a smuggler.

General Washington was instructed by the court to write a letter criticizing Benedict for his crimes. Even though Benedict was in fact guilty, he was very hurt that his old friend and supporter would actually write the letter. It made him more determined than ever to help the British.

André and Benedict came up with a plan. Benedict would get General Washington to give him command of West Point, a key American fort on the west bank of the Hudson River, north of New York City. Then Benedict would turn that fort over to Clinton, André, and the British.

West Point

In June 1780, André agreed to pay Benedict most of what he asked for.

In July, General George Washington surprised Benedict. He offered him a very important assignment. The general did not know about his deal with André, of course, and believed that Benedict was still loyal. He asked Benedict to take command of a large part of the Continental Army as it prepared for battles in the months ahead.

Benedict turned down the assignment and, just as he had planned with André, asked for command of the West Point fort instead. Washington was surprised but gave his general what he wanted.

Benedict wrote to André and arranged for the British officer to come ashore and meet with him. This was a big risk for André. If he was caught out of uniform in American territory, he could be put to death as a spy. (Soldiers in uniform were only taken prisoner, not killed.) Clinton had ordered him to always wear his uniform and to avoid going into American territory.

On September 21, 1780, on the banks of the Hudson River not far from West Point, John André stepped off a rowboat that had taken him from the British ship HMS *Vulture*. He was soon met nearby by Benedict Arnold.

CHAPTER 9
A Fateful Meeting

It was well after midnight when André and Benedict met. By the light of their lanterns, they talked about the plans Benedict could provide and how the British might use them. André said

that the British would pay six thousand British pounds (more than one million dollars today) but that he would try to get that amount up to twenty thousand pounds.

Following the meeting, André thought he would immediately return to his ship. However, after he had come ashore, American gunboats fired on the *Vulture*, which had to quickly sail away. That meant André was stranded. He had to stay another day, hiding in American territory but protected by Benedict.

When Benedict felt it was safe, he gave André six folded letters. He had written up a plan of attack for the British to use and drawn diagrams of the fort at West Point. It was everything the British would need to capture this important part of America's defenses. He told André to put the papers with the plans for West Point in his boots. With this act, Benedict Arnold had truly become a traitor to his country.

Benedict had a plan to get André safely back to the British side of the river. He asked his friend Joshua Hett Smith to guide André south through American territory toward New York City, which was controlled by the British. He wrote out passes to show to any American soldiers they met on the way. But he also told André to change out of his uniform. André did this, even though Clinton had told him not to.

Joshua Hett Smith

Smith and André rode their horses south. But not long into the journey, Smith left André to continue on alone. The British spy carried a pass from Benedict that he hoped would get him safely through American lines.

On September 23, some hunters stopped André in the woods and demanded to know who he was. The men were members of a patriot scouting party. André thought they were Tories on patrol in British territory, so he said that he was a British officer. When he realized his mistake, he said he was only joking. But the men did not believe him.

André was thoroughly searched. The men looked through all of his clothes. Finally, they told him to pull off his boots. Inside, they found papers and plans that looked very important, indeed. They showed details of the defenses at the military fort at West Point.

The men took André to a nearby American outpost run by Colonel John Jameson, who quickly wrote a letter to the commander at West Point telling him that they had captured a spy. The commander who received that letter was Benedict Arnold himself, the man who had secretly given André the plans!

At the same time, Jameson sent the six folded letters to General Washington, along with a note about how they had been found. As André was being captured, it happened that Washington was on his way to inspect West Point and see his old friend Benedict. He had sent some of his aides ahead. One was Alexander Hamilton, who would later become secretary of the treasury. This group of Washington's officers was having breakfast with Benedict at his house when the message to Benedict from Jameson arrived.

Benedict was shocked to see the news of André's capture, but he hid his surprise from

Washington's officers. He knew that André could reveal Benedict's betrayal. Without showing the officers the note, he got up suddenly from the table and told the men he had urgent business at the fort. He ran upstairs to see Peggy. He told her André had been captured and that he must flee.

Benedict rode on horseback to the waterfront.
He forced a pair of rowers to take him to the
Vulture, which the night before had been able to
sail farther down the river. He stepped aboard the
British ship to safety.

Less than an hour later, General Washington rode up to Benedict's house. The note from Jameson to Washington also arrived, along with the captured plans. Washington realized, to his horror, what had happened. "Arnold has betrayed me," he said. "Whom can we trust now?" Benedict's disloyalty was clear. The hero of Saratoga and one of America's best generals was guilty of treason.

While Benedict sailed to New York City, John André was put on trial as a spy. The evidence was overwhelming. He had been caught red-handed with details about the fort at West Point. He was convicted and sentenced to be hanged.

André was dead, but Benedict was still alive. News of Benedict's crimes swept across the colonies. After the first stories came out, Americans were shocked and angry at what he had done. Some people created an effigy—a stuffed dummy that looked like Benedict—hung it up, and set it on fire. His family headstones in a Connecticut cemetery were knocked over.

Washington's officers did not think Peggy Arnold was involved with the treason. Few thought that a woman would do such a thing.

They let her go, and she was able to escape with their children to join Benedict in New York City. For his part, Benedict continued to defend his actions. In October 1780, he wrote a letter called "To the Inhabitants of America" that was published in many newspapers.

In the letter, he tried to explain why he had sold the West Point plans to the British. He blamed some colonial leaders for abusing their positions. He worried that the new country of the United States had too close a relationship to France, which had come to help in the battle against the British. In the end, he really did not apologize at all.

In fact, he said he would treat anyone who disagreed with him "with contempt and neglect."

CHAPTER 10
Arnold's Shame

As part of his deal with André, Benedict was made an officer in the British Army. He then took command of British troops that fought in Virginia and Connecticut, near his old hometown.

In one battle in Connecticut, Benedict directed his troops to kill as many "rebels"—American soldiers—as they could. Many called it one of the most brutal battles of the war.

Then in October 1781, the British Army surrendered to the Continental Army after the Battle of Yorktown in Virginia. Benedict's side had lost the war.

Benedict had to escape America completely, since the victorious Continental Army was still hoping to capture him. He left for London, taking Peggy and his children with him. A year earlier, their son Edward had been born. Together, Benedict and Peggy would have five children of their own, in addition to Benedict's three older children.

In London, Benedict tried to fit in, but he never found his place in British society. He was still an American. And even though he had worked for them, some British people looked down on him for his treason.

In 1785, Benedict moved to Canada, which was still a British colony, and went back to his old work of running a trading ship.

In 1794, he was sailing in the Caribbean again, buying West Indian goods to sell back in Canada. By this time, Great Britain was in a war with France. A French ship near the island of Guadeloupe captured Benedict's ship, and he was taken prisoner. The French captain recognized Benedict, even though he had given a false name. Benedict realized that he would be turned over to the Americans, who still wanted to put him on trial for the crime of treason.

Late one night, Benedict pulled some wooden boards from the walls of the cabin where he was being kept aboard the ship. Perhaps thinking like the adventurous boy he had once been, he made a small raft from them and slipped over the side.

He paddled the raft to a rowboat, which he stole to make his way to the safety of a British-owned ship.

Not long after, Benedict's wife and children left their home in Canada and met him in London. Benedict himself became too sick to return to a life at sea. He ran his shipping business from England until he died on June 14, 1801.

To this day, Benedict Arnold remains the most famous and notorious traitor in American history. On a chapel wall at the United States Military Academy West Point, the names of the famous generals of the American Revolution are listed but not Arnold's. Because he had dishonored his name, only his rank and birth date appear.

On the farm where he was wounded in Saratoga, now part of a National Historic Park, a monument to his bravery was put up. But it does not show his face or his name. Instead, the stone carving shows only a left leg in a stirrup, wearing a long leather riding boot. Benedict's left leg was wounded in battle and is remembered well. But the man to whom that leg belonged will never receive honor in the United States of America.

Timeline of Benedict Arnold's Life

1741	Born in Norwich, Connecticut
1752	Sent to boarding school in Canterbury, Connecticut
1754	Becomes an apprentice at the Lathrops' apothecary
1761	Opens his own shop in New Haven, Connecticut
1767	Marries Margaret Mansfield
1768	Son Benedict born
1769	Son Richard born
1772	Son Henry born
1775	Chosen to lead local militia
	Helps capture Fort Ticonderoga from the British
1777	Wounded while helping win the Battles of Saratoga
1778	Named military governor of Philadelphia
1779	Marries Peggy Shippen
1780	Sells plans for West Point to British spy John André
1781	Moves to London to escape capture by victorious Americans
1785	Moves to Canada to run shipping business
1801	Dies in London

Timeline of the World

1735 — Swedish scientist Carl Linneaus invents way to name animals and plants

1741 — Danish sea captain Vitus Bering is the first European to reach Alaska

1755 — British author Samuel Johnson publishes his famous *Dictionary of the English Language*

1756 — Seven Years' War begins in Europe

1769 — James Watt invents and patents his famous steam engine

1773 — The Sons of Liberty dump British tea in Boston Harbor, in an event that came to be known as the Boston Tea Party

1776 — American colonies publish their Declaration of Independence

1781 — American colonial forces win final battle in the American Revolutionary War

1783 — Montgolfier brothers fly first hot-air balloon in France

1787 — United States Constitution signed

1792 — French Revolution ends monarchy in France

1799 — While occupying Egypt, Napoleon's soldiers find the Rosetta Stone

1807 — The US Congress passes a law banning the import of slaves

— US vice president Aaron Burr is arrested in Alabama for treason

Bibliography

*Books for young readers

*Burgan, Michael. *Benedict Arnold: American Hero and Traitor.*
Mankato, MN: Capstone Press, 2007.

*Dell, Pamela. *Benedict Arnold: From Patriot to Traitor.*
Minneapolis, MN: Compass Point Books, 2005.

*Fritz, Jean. *Traitor: The Case of Benedict Arnold.*
New York: PaperStar, 1981.

Philbrick, Nathaniel. *Valiant Ambition: George Washington,*
Benedict Arnold, and the Fate of the American Revolution.
New York: Viking, 2016.

Randall, Willard Sterne. *Benedict Arnold: Patriot and Traitor.*
New York: William Morrow, 1990

*Sheinkin, Steve. *The Notorious Benedict Arnold: A True Story of*
Adventure, Heroism, & Treachery. New York: Roaring Brook,
2010.